Deborah Sampson

Her Childhood

Pamela Archambault

Deborah Sampson

Her Childhood

Pamela Archambault

This is a portrait of Deborah Sampson-Gannett
She was a Revolutionary War soldier

Library of Congress Control Number:

ISBN: 9798399490373 *given out by KDP*

First edition, 2023

Book design by the gloria jainchill
Front cover and photographs by gloria jainchill

Author: Pamela Archambault

Email: parcha5237@aol.com

Printed by Kindle Direct Publishing
An amazon.com Company
https://www.kdp.amazon.com
amazon.com, Inc., P. O. Box 8226,
Seattle, WA 98109-1226

Available from Amazon.com and other retail outlets,
online stores and other bookstores

A 1770's area home, not Deborah Sampson's

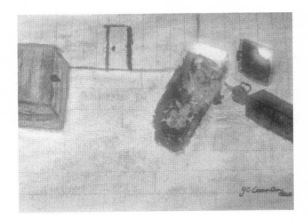

Room where Deborah birthed the idea of fighting in the
Revolutionary War as a soldier, the 'Blooming Boy'

DEDICATIONS
Cunningham is Pam's maiden name.
To my parents who ignited the joy of reading
and writing. To my grandmother who was my
inspiration and encouraged me along the way.

ACKNOWLEDGEMENTS
The River Runs Through It writing group who
pushed and pulled me through it.

To Richard, my nephew, who got my thoughts
going.

ABOUT THE COVER
The cover is a watercolor painting designed by
Pam and painted by gloria cassandra-Jainchill.
It depicts the room where becoming a
Revolutionary War soldier was birthed.

Deborah Sampson and Paul Revere knew each
other and looked out for each other.

Listen, my children, and you shall hear
Of the midnight ride of Paul Revere,
On the eighteenth of April, in Seventy-five;
Hardly a man is now alive
Who remembers that famous day and year.

He said to his friend, "If the British march
By land or sea from the town to-night,
Hang a lantern aloft in the belfry arch
Of the North Church tower as a signal light,

One, if by land, and two, if by sea;
And I on the opposite shore will be,
Ready to ride and spread the alarm
Through every Middlesex village and farm,
For the country folk to be up and to arm."

Table of Contents

A plaque honoring Deborah Sampson

Chapter 1: Baby Is Born

Aunt Hannah and Cousin Ruth came in the morning to help Mother as she gave birth. It was made clear by the aunties that children were to stay outside. They went to the barn and began chores. Deborah was very excited about the baby being born. Upon entering the barn, she started following her oldest brother Jonathan pestering him about being an older sister.

Deborah was the first to hear the baby cry, a very high-pitched scream, which slowly grew faint. She looked at Jonathan bent over, milking the cow. "The baby cried!"

He teased her. "You're a silly goose. Of course, I heard the baby cry."

Disobeying Auntie's orders to stay away, most of the children left and ran to the house immediately after hearing the baby's first wail. Annoyed they all went, Jonathan looked up at Deborah and smiled. "Thanks for staying. The milking must get done, or the cows will dry up, and they'll be no milk."

Deborah added. "Our family needs this milk."

Letting out a long sigh, she handed another empty pail to her brother. He sat on a stool and skillfully milked the waiting cow. Jonathan grinned up at her and reassuringly said," A few minutes for this cow to be finished. This is the last one."

She was anxious thinking about missing out on seeing the baby. They did all the morning chores by themselves without any help. Jonathan started milking the cows late because of them leaving. Ephraim came running back into the barn. He looked and saw Jonathan was at the front of the barn finishing to milk the last cow. He grinned sheepishly. "Sorry, I left."

Deborah rolled her eyes at her brother Jonathan who said to him. "I could have used your help."

Jonathan finished, and they left the barn. Deborah skipped alongside Ephraim and Jonathan, carrying the bucket full of milk. Hannah was waiting for them and swung open the door. A smile lit up her face. It was the first time Deborah remembered feeling happy since her grandmother died. Her thoughts flew to her father. He had left on a ship a month before Grandmother's death. Father made a promise to return before the baby was born. The baby had arrived, and yet, no father. However, now Deborah thought she had a reason to feel happy.

Life seemed better knowing a baby had been born.

It had been a few weeks since baby Sylvia was born. The mother remained in bed very weak. Next to her bed was the wooden cradle holding the baby. Hannah was trying to care for Mother and the infant. Deborah was sure her father would return home soon and help them. The days had grown longer and warmer. Summer was near, and he had not come home to his family.

Deborah noticed that Hannah's face had turned crimson. She was grabbing the threshold of Mother's bedroom door. She burst into tears, looking at Deborah, and choked out. "Father is not coming back to us."

Deborah was with little Nehemiah when Hannah appeared in the doorway. The constant jabbering from her little brother seized. Mother's sobbing surged throughout the house. Hannah was looking straight at Deborah, and their eyes met. She felt her skin prickle and grow chilly.

Hannah said, "Something awful happened. Father is dead. The mother got a letter this morning. He's gone."

Jonathan came walking into the parlor at the same moment Hannah had spoken to her. He was shocked by what he had just heard. His bottom lip started quivering. Hannah frantically looked at her brother and repeated. "Father is dead. He died in a shipwreck. "

She inhaled a deep breath. Barely audible and hoarse from the continuous crying and ran to Johnathan. "Get Uncle Nehemiah. He will know what to do!"

Jonathan turned around and ran to the door, yelling back to Hannah. "I know where he is. Uncle Nehemiah is at Sproats' tavern. He's working there."

The tavern was a meeting place for men in the surrounding towns. The news of Father's death spread quickly through the villages. Jonathan brought Uncle Nehemiah back to the house, who passed Deborah sitting on a bench near Mother's bedroom. Deborah swallowed her tears once she saw her uncle.

Before entering Mother's room, he suddenly turned around. "Now, each of you must go to bed. Everyone except Jonathan."

Jonathan, the oldest Sampson child, stood near Mother's bedroom door. "You all heard Uncle

Nehemiah; it is time to go to bed. We need to be brave. Go to bed."

They all obeyed Uncle Nehemiah's orders.

Deborah got up from the bench and walked toward Hannah and Ephraim. She said, "Let's go to the loft and get in our beds."

In the morning, Jonathan gathered them all around the parlor table. He looked at each of them, one at a time, not saying anything. Raking his right hand through his wavy blonde hair, he said, "Uncle Nehemiah talked to me a long-time last night after all of you went to bed. He explained to me what happens to children without parents."

Feeling her cheeks grow hot, Deborah almost got ill thinking about having no parents. "What do you mean, Mother is not dead? What happened to our mother?"

"Mother is very sick and can't take care of us. She isn't getting better since having the baby. Uncle Nehemiah said a town meeting is going on in a few days about our family. Uncle Nehemiah is going to represent our family since our father is dead. He is responsible for making sure we have a home."

The next few days passed slowly for Deborah. Hannah's chit-chat with young Nehemiah turned cruel. The conversations with him were hateful. The little boy had no idea what his sister meant when Hannah said that Mother was sick and didn't want her children. And it was a burden for Deborah as she heard the mean words.

Deborah grabbed Hannah's arm, who just finished giving baby Nehemiah a bath, and said, "stop being so mean."

Hannah looked back at Deborah. She hissed out her words like a snake," You are just a little girl. Don't you ever tell me what to do!" Hannah fumed.

She wagged her pointer-finger in Deborah's angry face.

Ephraim got up from stoking the fire and spit out furiously. "Jonathan just left the house to see our uncle, and I'm in charge. If you little girls want to fight, then go outside."

Jonathan met in the tavern with Uncle Nehemiah after the town meeting. He told Jonathan. "The decision about the Sampson family has been made. The vote was made hastily. You all must leave in two days. Each child will live with relatives. Except for young Nehemiah, the baby, and your mother. They will live in my farmhouse."

Jonathan sniffled, wiping his shirt sleeve across his face looking up into his uncles' distraught face, and said, "I can tell them in the morning."

He ran out of the tavern and went home.

Deborah Sampson was sent to live with her cousin Ruth as a young child after her father died. Ruth became her mother and teacher.

Chapter 2: The Town Meeting

They all knew their brother went to Sproat's Tavern last night to meet with Uncle Nehemiah. Jonathan was sitting in the parlor the following morning. Eventually, his younger brother Ephraim and sister Hannah came into the room. Deborah already stood beside Jonathan, watching him stoke the fire. Nehemiah and baby Sylvia were in the bedroom they shared with Mother. The little ones were asleep, and Mother had refused to leave the bedroom. They all remained silent. Jonathan's started to speak, and his voice cracked. He began shaking. Hannah gripped Jonathan's hand, trying to calm his nervousness. After a few seconds, he was better. Jonathan cleared his throat to speak, lowering his voice. He said, "All of you know last night was the town meeting about us. All the townsmen voted at the meeting about our family. Uncle Nehemiah told me that they have decided we must leave Mother and live with relatives who agreed to take us."

Deborah cried, "No, I won't go."

Her mind filled with thoughts. "Mother was not allowed to vote at the town meeting about taxes and was stopped from selling eggs since she did not have a husband. Mother came home upset that women could not vote or try to support their families. Now, these same men are ripping apart our family. How could they decide such a horrible thing?"

Hannah dropped Jonathan's hand and stood directly in front of him. Putting each hand on her hip, Hannah looked just like Mother and declared. "How can those mean men vote to decide our fate?"

Hannah plopped herself into Mother's rocker, burying her face in her hands. She suddenly spun around and glared at Jonathan. Indignantly she screamed. "Those men are awful. Why don't women matter."

The helpless faces of Deborah and her siblings watched Hannah yell at Jonathan. Ephraim let out a helpless snivel. He came from behind Hannah, patting her shoulder, and said, "Hannah, it is not his fault."

Jonathan stood at the end of the table. He said with tears on top of his pale, freckled cheeks, scanning his siblings' faces. "We are all to be farmed out with our relatives. Uncle Nehemiah is not sure who will take us. He said it must be this way. It is the law."

Ephraim moved away from his sister and ran to the door. He flung it open and yelled. "No one can take me if I run away." He disappeared out the door, leaving it wide open.

Within a few minutes, Ephraim returned. Johnathan's distraught face turned encouraged, seeing his prompt return. He rushed to Ephraim and slapped his back, "I need your help with the morning chores. We can talk in the barn."

The two brothers walked silently side by side out the door. Hannah and Deborah spent most of the morning together, weeding the garden and gathering vegetables. Hannah fussed and fumed the entire time. She whined. "Tomorrow, Uncle Nehemiah comes to tell us how we get split up."

Deborah took a rotten tomato and flung it against the wooden shed attached to the house and said, " It can't be true."

Hannah replied. " Yes, it is the truth, and you know it. Jonathan would not lie, and Uncle Nehemiah said it was decided by all the townsmen."

Uncle Nehemiah and his wife came the next day. Mother sat in her rocker beside the fireplace. Hannah was busy changing baby Sylvia's clout. Little Nehemiah's chubby face lit with glee the second they came through the door. Young Nehemiah was speaking gibberish while the mother kept repeating words to correct him. Deborah was not happy to see them and was puzzled by her mother's devotion, only focused on her brother. Deborah thought. "She must know we all have to leave. Why doesn't she care?"

Deborah stood in front of her Aunt and Uncle. "Are you here to take us away?"

"Hush, child," Mother demanded and gave her brother an apologetic look.

Uncle Nehemiah took off his hat, handing it to his wife, beads of sweat sparkling on his forehead. They walked to the table, and Uncle Nehemiah pulled out a chair for Aunt Hannah to sit. She kept looking at the children. He said crossly. "Hannah, you may sit."

Agitated by his demand Aunt Hannah ignored him and went to help Mother come to the table. Uncle Nehemiah remained at the table, wiping sweat from his brow. He scanned the room with bloodshot eyes. Uncle Nehemiah said. "It's time for our family to talk. All of you get to the table and listen."

He placed a red lace bag on the table and withdrew out an old jar. He saw the children all recognize the tiny glass jar. "This small honeypot once belonged to Grandmother Bradford," Uncle Nehemiah said with reverence.

"Grandmother shared her last story in this room. He raised his arm high in front of him while grasping the old jar. She said all her prayers, hopes, and dreams for each of you while holding this empty jar. She is a beloved Grandmother. Although she may not be here today, it is critical to remember her love and faith in God," said Uncle Nehemiah.

He shut his eyes and folded his hands in front of him as if to pray. After a few seconds, his eyes opened. Uncle Nehemiah spoke in his church voice.

"Each of you will live with relatives, not strangers. Your mother, baby Sylvia, and little Nehemiah will stay in our home. And other family members will come tomorrow morning to take one of them home with them, pack tonight.

Mother's eyes had tears, and finally, she began to speak. "Go pack your things and get to bed. Uncle Nehemiah is helping our family. We need to be grateful."

The following morning, each child was retrieved by family members. Deborah was the last Sampson child to leave. She wondered what would happen if no one came to take her to a new home. Mother would not leave the bedroom all morning, and Deborah went from the empty parlor with dread. She climbed the wooden ladder to the loft, feeling left behind. Her few things were wrapped in Grandmother's old shawl. For some reason, she thought she had to take the bundle of possessions with her to the loft. She held tight to her belongings; a dress, two woolen socks, and a hairpin stuck in a brush packed in the shawl. She reached the top of the ladder and swung her bundle onto the floor of the loft. She then climbed off the ladder and looked at the room. She looked at her straw mattress on the girl's side of the attic. Deborah mumbled to herself.

"Only a few stains from being sick to show for my life here."

The boy's side was empty except for a thin sheet hung on a rope, dividing the space that once held her brothers. She heard the front door open and the deep voice of Uncle Nehemiah. She wiped the tears from her eyes, and a wave of nausea hit her stomach. She bolted to the corner wrenching on the straw mattress a final time. She felt better. While climbing down the ladder, she felt a hand

on her head and turned to see Uncle Nehemiah.
" I thought I heard you get sick up there" Uncle
Nehemiah asked.

Deborah sadly replied. "I am fine."

"I have the wagon ready. It takes until noon to
get to Cousin Ruth's farmhouse in
Middleborough."

She turned toward him, elated. " Cousin Ruth
wants me?"

"Of course, she does" Uncle Nehemiah said
while taking her bundle of things she was
struggling to hold.

Deborah finished coming down the ladder from
the loft. She followed her Uncle into the parlor.

Deborah was surprised to see her mother in the
rocker holding baby Sylvia. Mother was too
weak to come out of her bedroom even as they
left with relatives. Deborah thought to herself,
"Mother finally came out of the room, just in
time to see me go."

Wondering about her future, she looked at
Mother, trying to memorize the moment. Mother
immediately began looking down at baby Sylvia.
Her small brother held onto the rocker's arm.

"Go say goodbye to your mother", Uncle Nehemiah instructed.

Deborah sadly shook her head no and took herself and her bundle to the front door. Uncle Nehemiah opened the door and grabbed the small bunch. He shrugged at his sister, smiled compassionately, and said, "She got that strong will from you."

A sad smile crossed Mother's face. He gently closed the door and led Deborah to the wagon. Deborah let out a heavy sigh of relief. "Mother had not noticed my things wrapped in grandmother's shawl."

Deborah thought to herself. Grandmother's shawl, the only thing she wanted to take, the keepsake seemed right.

Uncle Nehemiah lifted her onto the wagon seat and climbed up beside her. "Where are my things?" Deborah asked him.

For the first time in days, he chuckled. "I put your cloths in your grandmother's shawl under the wagon seat. So, you would be sitting on top of your things." This small attempt at a joke, for some reason, made Deborah feel guilty for taking the shawl. She let out a sheepish laugh.

A statue of Deborah Sampson,
Considered a Massachusetts's heroine.

Chapter 3: Off We Go

They began their trip to Cousin Ruth's, enjoying each other's company and her guilty feelings left. She often wondered if her Uncle resembled Grandfather Bradford, who had died the same year her parents were married.

She was curious and did not hesitate to ask him. He smiled his gentle smile, "I sure do. I have heard folks remark that I look like my father."

Deborah found her Uncle to be a great man. She looked up, tipping her bonnet to shield her eyes from the sun, " I think you are a good Uncle."

Deborah looked back and was surprised to see only the woods behind them. She looked back at this point to see her home in Plympton one last time. Now it was soon gone from her view. She held her breath for a moment, then decided. " It's not my home anymore."

The road they traveled on was busy at times. Uncle Nehemiah nodded a friendly hello when wagons passed. She liked how good he was to everyone, and he was also the wisest person in her entire family.

A few cold raindrops hit Deborah's face, they stung her as the rain turned to sleet. The trees became decorated with a glaze of ice. Uncle Nehemiah withdrew an old blanket from under the wooden seat and told Deborah to wrap it around her shoulders. "Hold on tight. Looks like this storm is getting worse."

It was the first time Deborah had ever felt hail. She lived her whole life near the coast and couldn't remember frozen rain.

Uncle Nehemiah looked down at Deborah, grinning. "Surprised at the cold rain? Look over there. See that farmhouse on the hill? That is Ruth Fuller's place. I am sure Cousin Ruth has supper ready. We will be there soon."

The ride with her Uncle, suddenly, felt awful. She was not sure what to think about Ruth and her farm in this land that had ice. A few minutes passed, and the sleet subsided. Patches of sun graced the pasture and made the grass glisten. Deborah felt her despair turn to a sense of wonder. Life had somehow become an exciting adventure. They rode up the winding dirt driveway to the large old farmhouse. It had been well cared for even though Ruth was living alone. Uncle Nehemiah said, " This place once held a dozen family members. It thrived, and folks came from far off to learn about farming from Ruth's father. Her father was my favorite Uncle, such an owlish man. There was much laughter, along with hard work. He made you feel like you were important. It was a great family."

Ruth Fuller was standing by on the front porch when they arrived. She waved cheerily at them. Deborah politely waved back. Uncle Nehemiah drove the wagon near the front porch where Ruth stood. "Hello, you two, welcome.

Deborah noticed Ruth looked like her mother, with the exception she was a bit slimmer and older.

Cousin Ruth said, "Nehemiah, put the wagon and horses in the barn."

She added, "The old red cow and the brood of chickens are still a nuisance."

"Thanks, I imagine those horses would appreciate some warm, dry shelter. Although it sounds like the barnyard is still bothersome to strangers."

They left Ruth on the porch, and they rode around the corner to the barn. Deborah looked around the barn fearing the mean red cow. Uncle Nehemiah chuckled. His blue eyes danced.

"Don't be afraid of the old cow. She is a sweet thing. The chickens are harmless birds too, just pesky."

The barn was attached to the back of the house. Uncle Nehemiah drove the wagon inside the barn. How surprising the sweet smell of hay calmed her spirit. Jumping down from the wagon, she saw an old reddish cow sauntering toward them. "Well, hello, Nellie," said Uncle Nehemiah.

The cow bowed her head down, looking at Deborah with warm brown eyes and nuzzled her shoulder. Deborah gave Nellie an affectionate hug and thought. "If that old cow loves it here, maybe I will too," Deborah thought to herself.

She helped Uncle Nehemiah unbuckle the horses and feed them the water-filled trough. The horses were settled near a stall of fresh hay. Uncle Nehemiah was hanging up the harness when Ruth opened a door near the barn's end and motioned for them to come. " Well, what do you think, time to go inside and get you settled?" Uncle Nehemiah asked Deborah.

"I'm ready," She quipped.

Uncle Nehemiah turned and waved to Ruth, standing in the doorway. She waited for them to make their way to the end of the barn where she stood. Turning around, she took them down a short dark hallway into the house. Bright sunlight greeted them as they entered the parlor. Surprised, Deborah blinked, adjusting her eyes to the intense light.

As her vision came into focus, she looked around with curiosity. "I've never been to such a beautiful home," she thought.

A massive wooden table had chairs on either side resting on a round, dark red braided rug covering the wood floor. A patchwork quilt was draped over a black rocker next to the stone fireplace. A small stool was beside the rocker, and a dainty teacup and saucer had a biscuit resting on a plate.

Deborah smelt the aroma of apple pie. As she went further into the parlor, more smells of meat and vegetables calmed her anxious stomach. Ruth had a stew simmering in a large cauldron in a stone fireplace. Uncle Nehemiah broadly grinned, "It smells just like my mother's stew. She taught you well," Uncle Nehemiah told Ruth.

"Yes, it is her recipe. I made plenty for you to bring home to your family," Ruth said.

Ruth's kindness overshadowed the sadness Deborah felt since she left her family home. Uncle Nehemiah tugged at Deborah's braids. " I think we all need to eat. It has been a long day."

They all enjoyed the meal together. Deborah listened as Ruth spoke to Uncle Nehemiah about her mother. She enjoyed learning details about her mother. After much reminiscing, Ruth looked at Deborah and said, "My goodness, you have not said a word. You certainly were hungry. Your plate is empty, not a scrap of food left for Miss Boots."

Deborah looked around and said, "Who is Miss Boots?"

Uncle Nehemiah hastily answered, "Has she been hiding all this time since we arrived? I thought the old cat died." He turned to Deborah. "Miss Boots is Ruth's cat."

Ruth spoke, "I suppose she is afraid. This old place is usually empty except for me."

They had finished the meal. Deborah knew it was time to clear the table and stood to reach for her plate and looked at Ruth. "Thank you for dinner."

Smiling, Ruth left the table. She walked over to the cauldron of stew hanging in the fireplace. "

Ruth looked right at Deborah and said, "Someday, I will show you how to make the stew-like your grandmother taught your mother and me. We were young girls, just like you," then she paused," Deborah, it is about time to show you to your room.

Uncle Nehemiah stood and said, "Cousin, that was a delicious meal. I better get back to Plymouth soon. Deborah can get acquainted with her new surroundings and you."

Ruth showed Deborah to the bedroom off the parlor. Uncle Nehemiah remained at the table. First, Deborah gathered the bundle she left near the hallway.

Ruth walked a short distance past the stone fireplace. Deborah's door to her bedroom was around the corner.

Deborah followed Ruth. She was stunned. She had a bedroom just for herself. "This bedroom is just for me," Deborah stated.

Ruth said. "My goodness, gracious. Yes, my dear."

The room had a reddish wooden dresser and a small vanity with an oval mirror above it. A cushion with rose-colored material was underneath the window. The bed was beside a narrow window and crisp white curtains that flapped in the evening breeze. Ruth rushed to the window and closed it. "Oh my, I forgot and left the window open. No wonder this room is cold." She laughed at her forgetfulness.

Deborah looked at the beautiful bedroom and said, "This is for me."

"Yes, Deborah, and my bedroom is right next to yours." Ruth sat on the bed and knocked on the wall. "Just knock on the wall if you need me," Ruth said.

Uncle Nehemiah peeked past Deborah's bedroom door. I better go, and Ruth, I would appreciate some help with that delicious stew you mentioned to bring home.

Ruth said, "Deborah, I'll go help your Uncle. You better get ready for bed. I will come back later to hear your prayers."

Uncle Nehemiah came into the bedroom. He said, " I think you will like it here."

"Thank you; I knew to trust you would find me a good home. Cousin Ruth is perfect." Deborah raced to her Uncle and hugged him.

At first, Deborah was scared to be alone. Ruth's constant cheerfulness helped soothe her nerves. The bedroom felt empty once she left. She sank into her feather bed. The crackle of her straw mattress in the loft had been horrible. "This is so comfortable- a soft feather bed just for me. " She spoke out loud.

Her sense of comfort turned quickly into fright. Something was crawling near her feet. It began to purr and wrapped around her ankles. Deborah thought. " I have a friend, the cat: Miss Boots."

Miss Boots, Ruth's gray cat, slept near Deborah's feet the entire night. She purred, and Deborah felt safe, feeling her warmness on her feet.

Ruth and Deborah spent every day together. Weeding the garden which gave each time to ask each other questions. Deborah thought Ruth was the kindest woman she ever met besides her Grandmother Bradford. They talked and talked. Each of them got along well. Deborah was curious. She blurted out, " Why haven't you married?"

"I think you would have been a good mother and wife," said Deborah.

Ruth's face turned pale. She held out her hand to Deborah. Two fingers were missing. Deborah stared at Ruth's hand, "I never noticed your two fingers were gone. What happened?"

Ruth told her the story: "I went to the river to get a bucket of water for my mother. After dipping the bucket in the river and turning around, a huge gray wolf snuck behind me. No sound came from my mouth when I tried to scream for help. The wolf bit his teeth into my side. The pain was horrible. I swung the heavy bucket of water, attempting to defend myself, and his sharp teeth sliced my hand open. More wolves came to attack me. I thought I was dying. My screams brought all the farmhands. They ran from the pasture and the barn and began killing the vicious animals. It took months to heal, and I could not walk." Teaching was the only way I knew to help children."

Ruth had taught school to girls and boys for the past sixteen years. Ruth told Deborah. " Most families only allowed boys to learn. "

Deborah looked mad, "If I had a daughter, it would be important for her to attend school."

Ruth nodded, enjoying her gumption. Reverend Conant at church gave Deborah a primer for her lessons. Ruth taught her to read and write. Deborah used the same slate that Ruth had used when she was a child. Ruth told Deborah, " Twenty years ago, girls were not allowed to learn outside of the home. My mother taught me what she knew, and that was that."

In the evenings, Ruth would read a bible verse to her, and Deborah recited it back. Ruth never got mad if she said the verse wrong. She smiled and said, "You tried, and can you try again?"

She liked it when Ruth was pleased. Her blue eyes sparkled with approval, and Deborah's entire being felt warm and full inside. While Deborah stoked the fire, she recited a few more verses. Ruth sat in her rocker and wrapped her shawl around her shoulders to stay warm and listened carefully as Deborah recited a verse.

After the candlelight grew dim, and Ruth could not see the words, she shut the well-worn Bible and said, "It is getting late. Time for this lady to rest, off to bed, dear."

At night, Ruth kissed Deborah's forehead. It signaled time to sleep. She would turn to Deborah and say, "I will see you in the morning."

Deborah went to her bedroom. At the same time, Ruth went to her bedroom. Deborah felt loved, even though Ruth never uttered the word.

A picture of farm life in Massachusetts.

Chapter 4: Ruth

A light breeze touched Deborah's face. She awoke to a bright spring morning and the sounds of young birds. They chirped, paused, and then returned to chirping.

Her body felt the warm sunlight that cascaded through her window. Deborah stepped on the heated floor from the sunshine. She gazed out the window and saw the lilac bush shake. A giant mother robin sat on a wire branch, and four small yellow beaks fought for a worm, which dangled from the mother's beak. Ruth rapped on her bedroom door, "Can I come in?"

"Yes, come see the baby birds," Deborah responded.

She rushed next to Deborah stood behind the stool. "Oh, my," Ruth said.

" Isn't it wonderful to watch the mother bird feed them?"

Ruth squeezed Deborah's shoulder. She turned to Ruth and said, "I am glad those little birds have food, but I would not like to eat worms. I think I would rather starve."

"Well, we have our breakfast to get ready."

Ruth said. "I have some good news. I asked your mother to visit. She was very excited. She is coming this afternoon."

Ruth noticed Deborah's sudden silence. "You do not look well."

"Oh, I am fine, just surprised. I thought Mother forgot about me," Deborah plainly stated.

An immediate expression of shock came across Ruth's face. "No, dear, you are her daughter."

Deborah winced, wishing her mother was not coming. " Your Uncle Nehemiah is bringing her.

We better get busy " Deborah weeded the garden and picked some vegetables, and Ruth tidied the house. The afternoon came, and Ruth had not called Deborah inside the house. She shrugged off her absence and continued to finish the morning chores. A queasiness hit her stomach, and she felt an urgent need to see Ruth. Deborah placed her basket of vegetables down. Deborah thought. "I better run; Ruth needs me."

With each step, she took a feeling of dread increased. She ran through the short dark hallway to the main house. In the parlor, she found Ruth slumped in her rocker. A teacup lay on the floor. Shards and slivers of glass were in a puddle of water near Ruth's black shoes. "Ruth, Ruth," Deborah cried. Deborah tried to lift Ruth's slumped body. Ruth's eyes remained open, and she stared a still stare. "No, no, no," Deborah screamed.

Deborah crumpled to the floor. She hugged Ruth's knees. Deborah cried and cried and then started to shiver. She heard voices and rushed to stand. Her vision sparkled, and the sounds echoed. Again, she tried to stand and wobbled until everything faded.

Strong arms lifted her and cradled her like an infant. Her eyes remained closed. The voice of her Uncle Nehemiah floated by her. She heard echoes to bed, bed, bed, then a soft blackness. She could smell lilacs. She felt the softness of her feather mattress. She recognized it was her room. Sleep drifted into her body. Miss Boots had curled her body beside her arm.

Light streamed through Deborah's bedroom window. She sat up in bed and looked at the quilt Ruth had made. It had been a birthday present when Deborah turned eight. She looked at the mirror across from her bed, and her thick sandy blonde hair was a tangled mess. Ruth had brushed her hair each morning. The mirror reflected the dress that she gave a few days ago. Ruth said that she had made the dress with her mother and saved it for her own child. The frilly dress needed altering. Deborah thought the dress was a bit fancy and too dainty for her. She had told Ruth, and she smiled at her, and she sighed. Ruth said. "I can fix it to suit you."

A lump grew in Deborah's throat as she longed for Ruth.

She heard Mother's high-pitched voice in the parlor. If only it was Ruth. She listened as her mother was speaking to Reverend Conant. Another man talked, and she recognized it was Uncle Nehemiah. He continued talking and then whispered. She could not hear him.

Deborah's temples throbbed, and the back of her neck ached. Something was heavy on her chest. She could not breathe and needed air. A gust of wind made her curtains flutter. She gulped the fresh air and escaped through her bedroom window. Revived by the fresh air, she ran down a well-traveled path to the brook that separated Ruth's pasture and the adjoining farm. The river had a flat stone that jutted out into the water. She had a secret place to think. She sat down on the huge rock, and tears streamed down her face. Trickled off her gray dress and plopped into the water. Small fish darted from underneath the boulder. She started to giggle, watching the tadpoles frantically scatter, her heart ached, and tears returned.

Deborah felt a light tap on her back and jerked with fright. She turned, seeing it was her older brother Ephraim. He looked at her with his lips drawn tight, "I know Ruth has died."

Deborah looked at her brother. She stood on the boulder and started to stumble. Ephraim grabbed her arm to steady her. Deborah looked up at her brother's solemn face and said, " I think hardship is my destiny."

Ephraim said. "You must be careful. I am glad you are okay. These woods are not safe."

A shadow of fear traveled across her face. Deborah then looked up at her brother and said, " I am not afraid.

Ephraim shook his head. He warned her, "If you get hurt because you are alone in the woods, it is your own fault."

She asked. "Yes, you are right. Can you walk with me to the house?"

"Sure," he said.

Deborah and Ephraim walked to the back of the house. Ephraim said, "I have to go. I think coming here might get me in trouble. The news about Ruth came from Mr. Thomas. He was at the tavern talking with Mr. Sproat, and I overheard Ruth died.

I better get back to the tavern."

Her brother left her in the back by the barn. She dreaded to go any further. She mustered her courage and went towards the house, reaching the back door. Deborah walked into the parlor. She saw her mother near the fireplace. Her back was to her, and Deborah walked right past her and toward her bedroom. Reverend Conant's face was pressed against her bedroom door. She heard him mumbling her name. He said, "Deborah, come out. It is the Reverend."

Uncle Nehemiah was behind him. The Reverend knocked on the door and looked over his shoulder. He saw her, Uncle Nehemiah's firm chin went downward, his mouth opened and quickly shut. The Reverend Conant briskly walked to Deborah. "My child, we thought you slept, and you were gone all this time."

She wanted to respond. No words left her lips.

Uncle Nehemiah just stood by the door. He said, "Thank the Lord, you are safe."

Mother scurried over to her, almost pushing the Reverend away from Deborah. Reverend Conant left them alone. Mother reached for her shoulder, shaking her, and questioned. "I thought you were in your bedroom. Where have you been?"

Deborah thought to herself, why hadn't her mother gone into the bedroom? She would have then known that she was not there. Deborah hoped her mother had come to reclaim her since Ruth had died. She only shook her instead of embracing her with a hug. Her mother told her, "I have made arrangements for you to live with someone else. Reverend Conant's helped find you a home."

Little did Deborah know that her mother could not support her.

A simple 1770's home

Chapter 5: The Widow Thatcher's House

The Reverend Conant looked at Deborah's mother and said, "May I have a word with the child?"

Her mother agreed and left them alone.

Reverend Conant told Deborah that the Widow Thatcher was married to Reverend Peter Thatcher who was the Pastor of the church before he came to preach.

The Reverend Conant looked woeful seeing Deborah's distraught face. She looked down at her feet, immediately noticing the old gray cat's snout poking out from underneath her bed. Miss Boots brought calmness to her distraught soul, not paying any mind to the Pastor talking, the cat kept her thoughts diverted.

Reverend Conant turned his head to see what caught Deborah's attention and saw the cat trying to hide. He then turned to Deborah. "I noticed the cat is watching you; she must be frightened."

Deborah nodded, lifted the cat from underneath the bed, hugged her and carefully placed her on top. She took her bag of things packed for her new home with the Widow Thatcher and leaned it against the wall. The cat gazed at the open window and jumped onto the windowsill.

Deborah grabbed her and put her on the floor. "She cannot go outside. She will get hurt."

Miss Boots scuttled under the bed.

The Reverend Conant shrugged his shoulders and grew stern. "Right now, you have a home. Don't worry about that foolish old cat. It is time for you to leave for the Widow Thatcher's home. Mr. Thomas has come to bring you to her house."

Deborah's eyes focused downward on her feet and obediently picked up the bag, focusing her anger on the handles, the knuckles of her clenched fist turned white. Reverend Conant's bushy eyebrows drew downward, and he walked out the door. Deborah was distraught, wishing Ruth had not died.

The Reverend Conant went and sat at the table next to Deborah's mother.

She noticed her Uncle Nehemiah was not there. Deborah remained standing. And would not look at her mother and thought, "Mother should have been with me in the bedroom instead of sitting at the table."

She turned, now focusing directly on her mother. "Where is my Uncle Nehemiah?"

"He took Cousin Ruth to the cemetery in Plymouth to be buried," her mother stoically replied.

Mr. Thomas sat in the rocker, withdrawing a cloth from his shirt pocket and he wiped his brow.

Deborah could only think of poor dead Cousin Ruth while looking at Mr. Thomas sitting in Ruth's rocker. He spoke to Deborah. "The Widow Thatcher lives a few miles from my farm."

Deborah felt some relief knowing that the Thomas family would be near to her. She had been to the church meetings in Middleborough with Ruth and found the Thomas family treated each other well. Deborah felt a burden to Cousin Ruth and was envious of the Thomas children having such a sweet mother. Sitting in church guilt often filled her thoughts wishing she had a kind mother like Mrs. Thomas.

Deborah was lost in her thoughts when the Reverend Conant said, "Deborah, it is time to go. The Widow Thatcher is expecting you and Mr. Thomas this afternoon."

Her mother remained at the table sobbing. Deborah walked past her looking straight ahead.

Mr. Thomas said only a few words to Deborah as they left Cousin Ruth's farm.

Riding in silence to her new home was fine. She thought to herself, "I am glad he is quiet."
They reached the Widow Thatcher's home after traveling only a few miles.

Deborah realized she had gone past the house every Sunday when she accompanied Ruth to church. The house looked in need of repairs, like she felt. The front yard had a few straggly bushes next to a gate. A dirt path led to the freshly painted white front door, the only part of the house that looked inviting.

"An old, old house. It looks lonely and sad except for the door."

"What did you say?" asked Mr. Thomas.

Before Deborah had time to answer, the front door popped open at the Widow Thatcher's home, a young woman came rushing down the dirt path to the wagon. She talked in a strange accent."

Good afternoon Mr. Thomas, this must be our Miss Deborah."

"Yes, my name is Deborah Sampson, are you the Widow Thatcher?"

"No, my dear," she retorted, I am the maid, Matilda. I look after her needs and such, she is inside and eager to meet you and see Mr. Thomas."

Deborah hopped down from the wagon, feeling woozy as soon as her feet hit the ground. Matilda came to her rescue and planted her arm firmly around her waist. Her quick action surprised Deborah.

"Thank you, Matilda."

"I could not let you slip, could I?" Matilda stated flatly.

Mr. Thomas grabbed Deborah's bag, and the three of them walked single file up the path. "Goodness, I am glad the cat did not flee, I left the door ajar."

Deborah started to have a glimmer of hope, and suddenly despair returned. "Miss Boots. What will happen to my cat?"

She thought. She stopped and gulped the tears from her eyes. Mr. Thomas walked ahead of Deborah through the door. A small room led to the parlor. She stayed behind him swallowing her tears. He never noticed her despair. Deborah obediently followed despite her troubled heart. The room was dim except for a few candles. The pleasant smell of bayberries was the aroma she had been accustomed to while living with Cousin Ruth. She was grateful the room was dim, and her tears hidden. Her eyes focused on an elderly, frail woman. The Widow Thatcher's frail body was hunched, standing in front of a small rocker. She didn't move away from the rocker.

Her hand trembled, holding the arm of the chair. Widow Thatcher smiled, her face displaying many wrinkles.

Mr. Thomas gently spoke, "Your kindness brings honor to your late husband's congregation."

The Widow's smile disappeared. "My late husband would do the same for this unfortunate child. Jeremiah thank you for bringing her. Please give your wife, Suzanne, my warmest regards."

Deborah timidly stepped into view from behind him. The Widow Thatcher remained near the rocker. Matilda suddenly appeared by her side and asked her, "Mam, can I get your cane?"

Widow Thatcher nodded. Matilda retrieved a wooden cane and handed it to her.

"Come to me, child," she wiggled her pointer finger at Deborah.

Deborah felt the intensity of her gaze and her body grew tense and rigid.

She took Deborah's hand. The older woman gazed at Deborah again. Their eyes met, and they both relaxed. "I am fortunate you came to live here." She patted her hand. "I can see in those eyes of yours that you are a kind girl. The granddaughter of Isaac Bradford, you come from exceptional people."

Deborah slowly stepped closer to the older woman to hear her soft voice.

"Your mother is a woman of respectable pedigree. I know that she has taught you well. Oh yes, I think your help is greatly needed."

The minute Deborah heard her mother praised; anger gushed through her veins. She hastily withdrew her hand.

"Poor, dead Cousin Ruth taught me to read and write," Deborah responded angrily, immediately feeling that she was rude as the words left her mouth.

"What did you say?" Asked the Widow Thatcher. "I can't hear if you mumble the words."

Deborah's face flushed. "Why can't I control my temper," Deborah said to herself. She could not talk. Her cheeks grew red hot with embarrassment and an uncomfortable silence swarmed around the room.

The Widow Thatcher broke the awkward silence. "Mr. Thomas, it was kind of you to bring Deborah under such sad circumstances."

Mr. Thomas bowed his head and raised it displaying a slight smile at the Widow Thatcher.

Deborah, still standing beside him, looked up and said, "Thank you, Mr. Thomas."

Mr. Thomas said. "Deborah, you now have a home. God has provided."

Mr. Thomas left her side and walked toward the entryway that led to the front door.

The Widow Thatcher pointed her slender finger

at Matilda and said, "It is time to bring Deborah to the room you two will be sharing."

Matilda looked at Deborah. "Well Missy, pick up your bag. I will show you to our room."

The thought of sharing a room with the mean servant was scary. Matilda's chin jutted upward with pursed thin lips aware of Deborah's disapproval. Remembering her manners, Deborah thanked the Widow Thatcher. Matilda stood impatiently waiting for Deborah to finish. A few minutes passed. Matilda led her to the bedroom and hastily stopped and turned around back towards the Widow Thatcher.

"Matilda, I wondered if you had forgotten me," said the Widow Thatcher.

"Oh no mam, I made supper earlier, with the girl arriving and such. She can help me finish the meal. Is Miss Deborah to eat tonight?"

Deborah was hungry. She stood by the bedroom entrance listening to them.

The Widow Thatcher seemed to be aware of Matilda's newfound bossiness.

"From now on Deborah will eat when I do. And she will help to prepare the meals. She is here to be my companion. Matilda, you are my servant. You can show Miss Deborah to the bedroom."

Matilda came back to Deborah at the bedroom doorway giving her a forceful shove into the room. Deborah almost fell until the mean woman grabbed her arm. Deborah and Matilda were facing each other. Deborah was not afraid, and that was the first thing she told her. "Don't ever push me again."

"Okay, Miss Deborah but be warned you can't be causing me trouble."

Deborah stared back at the vicious women and said nothing. She refused to fight.

The battle ended as if nothing had happened. Deborah walked further into the room. The bedroom room had two small windows. A little sunlight entered the room. A bed was under one of the windows with a chair near a tall bureau, and the other bed was near the door. A bureau was beside the bed near the door. Matilda pointed at the bed near the doorway. "This bed is mine. I must be able to hear and help the Widow Thatcher needing anything. Remember, this is my bed. You must never touch it."

"I won't!" Deborah promised.

She had dreaded living with the old woman and never imagined she would have a mean-spirited housekeeper.

She missed Cousin Ruth and was sorry she had not appreciated her constant kindness.

Deborah thanked God for Ruth's life and how much she had taught her. She missed Ruth, her teachings about God's promises which became her lifeline of hope. "I will not let Mean Matilda steal my joy. I am good like Ruth taught me."

Deborah emptied the small satchel filled with her things onto her bed. A pair of woolen socks, hairbrush, hairpin, and a necklace. And Grandmother's shawl. She also found a few more things she had not remembered packing: pie crimper, two solid white candles and the candle holder she had kept on her night chest. Wrapped in tissue was the fancy-dress Cousin Ruth gave Deborah. She wondered who packed these things?"

A wave of guilt hit Deborah knocking her onto the bed while her tears stung her tired eyes. "Oh no, thought Deborah what will happened to Ruth's cat?"

She heard a faint noise near her head and opened teary eyes to a blur of yellowish fur.

Matilda poked her curly head into the doorway. "I see that old cat found you. The Widow Thatcher said that you could care for her old cat."

Deborah smiled and scratched the old cat behind her furry ear. The cat purred and wrapped a paw around her wrist.

Matilda remained in the doorway clicking her mouth with disgust.

"You keep that old cat away from me and my things."

Matilda and her blazing red curly head had disappeared.

Deborah held the cat snug to her cheek and whispered, "You best keep away from mean Matilda."

She sat on the bed and cuddled the old cat who purred with contentment. The cat climbed in Deborah 's open arms licking salty tears off her face.

Matilda poked her head in the bedroom doorway and ordered, "I expect you for supper at four. Widow Thatcher has tea at that time too. You must be at the meals on time, or you will not eat. Those are my rules, and Widow Thatcher has also agreed."

Matilda stood inside the bedroom doorway with her hands on her hips.

Deborah realized at that moment that Matilda ran the household.

She took her meals with the Widow and helped her eat. Deborah read to the Widow each afternoon and wrote some letters. The Widow was delighted by her excellent penmanship and remarked, "Such beautiful work."

"My cousin Ruth was a teacher, she taught me to read, write and count," Deborah said proudly.

"Such an elegant woman was Ruth Fuller. It was sad to hear of her death. I knew Ruth would raise a fine girl. The minute Reverend Conant told me of your homelessness, I said, please bring her to live with me, and here you are."

She held the letter Deborah had written and tucked it into a small drawer of the table beside her rocker. Two teacups were at the top of the table. "We can write more tomorrow. It's time for afternoon tea."

Matilda appeared from the shadows and brought the late afternoon teapot. Holding a platter, Deborah watched her efficiently prepare the two dainty teacups. A floral-patterned porcelain plate held several biscuits. The Widow Thatcher's eyes lit up, and she smiled up at Matilda, "How lovely, thank you, Matilda."

Matilda looked at Deborah with a nasty gloat then she turned her head at the Widow Thatcher. The servant's face erupted in a tremendous smile placing the tray on the table beside her chair.

The days with the Widow became filled with all the chores that Matilda thought Deborah should do to earn her keep. The Widow Thatcher became ill and spent every day in bed. It was apparent to the Reverend Conant that Deborah could not live there.

Again, he found a new living arrangement for Deborah.

Chapter 6: Indentured

Deborah walked in the front door that Mr. Thomas held open and moved quickly to get away from the cold night air. The house was deathly quiet, not full of life like she had imagined. Mr. Thomas shut the door and stepped in front of her passing the bag of things she had brought from the Widow Thatcher's house. She saw Mrs. Thomas coming towards her. She silently guided her to the attic bedroom.

The wind wrapped around the farmhouse. Each gust sent a chill throughout Deborah's body. She remained awake feeling cold and abandoned and wished the night would end. How often had she listened to the wind howl, somehow, this was different. She thought. "I can't get attached to this family and must guard my heart."

Ruth had died and the kindly Widow Thatcher. Deborah felt their love, and she loved them. They both gave her a home when life had seemed hopeless. Life again looked impossible, every adult she loved, died. She wondered if her life would be an endless sea of hardships. Her thoughts turned to her father, helplessly swallowed by the sea.

She had known the Thomas family because they also attended the same Congregational church when she lived with the Widow Thatcher and Cousin Ruth. Deborah again reasoned with herself. This family needs help as much as I need a home. The Thomas family had five sons to raise, and a new baby would be born any day. She pondered for a moment and wondered why her mother had not claimed her after the Widow Thatcher died. She wondered why mother had cast her out to the Thomas family and not taken her home. She was an indentured servant girl until the age of eighteen. Just the thought made her heartache. She was indentured, bound out, the words sounded harsh just like the screeching wind.

Deborah looked toward the window, hugging her pillow, as the full moon shone in a cloudless sky. Stars happily twinkled as if nothing was wrong. She had not noticed the desk under the small window in her makeshift bedroom in the loft. The slivers of light from the moon revealed it. The outline of several books on top of the desk created butterflies in her stomach. Hope touched her soul and landed lightly. She was comforted and thrilled at the same time. She carefully crept from the bed, and held her breath, and tip-toed toward the desk. Something let out a loud groan. She wondered where the noise had come from and rushed back to her bed. A few minutes passed, and the sound repeated itself. Deborah threw the quilt over her head.

A woman's voice spoke softly from beside her bed. Deborah opened her eyes, pulled the quilt down, the dim twilight revealed the shadowy image of Mrs. Thomas. "The day starts early. I will see you downstairs."

"Yes, mam," Deborah answered, relieved she was not a ghost.

Mrs. Thomas lit a candle on a small chest near Deborah's bed.   Deborah's eyes adjusted quickly. She looked toward the window above the desk and smiled to herself. She threw her smock on over her head.

"My shoes, where did I put them?" She bent down beside the bed and retrieved them. Deborah joined Mrs. Thomas in the main room.

The smell of bread hung in the air. Deborah saw several loaves on the table. Mrs. Thomas turned from the stone fireplace and greeted Deborah with a sweat-drenched face. She remembered that her mother looked like that before her sister was born. Mrs. Thomas needed her help her waist was large and she was exhausted. Deborah attempted a weak smile, Mrs. Thomas had already turned her attention back to the stove.

Within seconds, Mrs. Thomas turned around and handed a large wooden bowl of porridge to Deborah. "You need to eat. You have many chores today. We cannot have your work suffer; you need food."

Deborah was hungry. She had not given any thought about food since her quick departure from the Widow Thatcher's home the previous evening.

"I am hungry, thank you, mam."

Mrs. Thomas looked right into Deborah's eyes, and reached for her chin," Child, you have the same hazel eyes as your grandmother Joanna Sampson. Ahh, the windows to the soul. She had such a kind heart."

She said this while letting out a reverent sigh.

Her comment reminded Deborah of her dead father, and she felt very awkward. She knew nothing of her grandmother Joanna. Mrs. Thomas spoke of her grandmother with such admiration. Dutifully, she finished her porridge while questions about this absent grandmother wandered through her mind.

Mrs. Thomas gave her a short time for her to eat. "In a few minutes, you may go to the barn, tend the chickens and gathered the eggs."

Deborah choked down her last spoon of lumpy porridge. "Yes, Mam."

Deborah was pleased to get away from the house. She found the basket for the eggs needed mending and made a mental note to fix it. A few chickens scattered across the barn chattering immediately after Deborah began pushing open the heavy wooden door. She hung the lantern on a wooden peg near the massive door. The barn came to life. Cows let out a welcoming moo. Deborah giggled, "Well, good morning."

"Home at last," she whispered to herself.

Deborah tried to get the last egg from an uncooperative chicken, when a young boy entered the barn.

Jeremiah ran to Deborah and jerked the angry bird off her nest, and she took the birds two eggs. " Birdy always puts up a fuss," he said gleefully.

"I better get these eggs back to your mother, I took too long, thanks."

She rushed to the barn door. The boy hollered when she whisked by him. "Jeremiah is my name. You must be Deborah Sampson."

"Yes, that would be me."

Chapter 7: Chores

Deborah hastily walked up the hill to the house carrying the basket filled with eggs. She was glad to have completed her first chore. From the corner of her eye, she caught the image of a skinny animal with a long tail and mumbled to herself. "A fox."

Mr. Thomas ran out of the shed beside the farmhouse. He was holding a musket. A large black dog raced past him headed towards the barn. Frightened, the fox dodged under some straggly bushes next to the barn. The small creature attempted to flee from its hiding place. Several shots from Mr. Thomas's musket shattered the early morning silence. The ill-fated fox tumbled lifelessly out of the bushes.

Abruptly one egg splattered onto Deborah's foot. Absorbed in watching what was happening, the basket she was holding had tilted to its side, and an egg had tumbled out hitting her shoe. Her arm jerked the basket upward before the other eggs could fall out. Annoyed by her carelessness, she feared her slimy shoe would reveal the ruined egg to Mrs. Thomas. Heavy-hearted, she slowly walked up the steep hill. The barking of the dog grew louder and seemed closer. Deborah jutted her chin forward as she saw the dog approaching her and continued to walk ignoring him, not about to repeat the same mistake of losing any more eggs. She firmly gripped the handle of the basket of eggs holding it against her stomach. The barking stopped, and the dog plunked himself in front of her. The dog looked exactly like Uncle Nehemiah's dog but much younger.

"Move out of my way," Deborah angrily demanded.

The dog stayed still except his tail wagging paying no attention to her order.

Pokerfaced, she swallowed her anger and moved forward attempting to bypass him. She felt the dog brush underneath her skirt and saw his furry black head bend, and she braced herself for a bite. Instead, she felt his rough tongue licking furiously at the egg splattered on her shoe.

A boy's voice came from behind, "I see you had trouble with Shep." Deborah recognized it was Jeremiah who was speaking.

The dog lifted his head from Deborah skirt and ran to Jeremiah. Relieved he had seen what happened, she turned with a grateful glance and said to Jeremiah, "I am glad he does not bite."

Jeremiah chuckled, "I think he will be your friend for the rest of your life after having his breakfast from your shoe."

Mr. Thomas came trudging up the hill behind them, dangling the dead fox out in front of him and yelled to his son. "Let your Ma know I killed the sneaky varmint that devoured her chicken."

Jeremiah ran back down to his father who handed him the dead fox and said, "You can skin him; I suspect his fur will make a fine pelt."

Deborah was farther ahead of them and reached the door of the farmhouse. She timidly opened the door and walked in to find two little boys stacking wood. Mrs. Thomas walked briskly to Deborah and took the basket of eggs. She looked at Deborah's sullen face and said, "I sent Jeremiah to help you with that persnickety chicken; I almost forgot how she could be so mean."

"Mam, he did help. I only have nine eggs, not ten as you told me to get."

A rush of air came into the room. Mr. Thomas went through the door into the parlor. Jeremiah came from behind him and then Shep wiggled between them both making a beeline for Deborah. Again, the dog started to lick her shoe. Mrs. Thomas's face looked puzzled. Deborah didn't utter a word. Her silence gave Jeremiah the opportunity to tell his mother why the dog was licking Deborah's shoe.

Jeremiah told the story about how Shep had caused one egg to accidentally fall out of the basket of eggs Deborah was carrying.

"It almost sounded ridiculous," Deborah thought as she heard him recount the scene.

The two young Thomas boys laughed at their older brother's story.

Mrs. Thomas's eyes shone with amusement as she looked at Deborah standing beside her. The dog raised his head from Deborah's shoe looking up, oblivious of what he had done. Mr. Thomas's remained near the door. His heavy eyebrows furrowed and commanded the mischievous dog. "Come here."

Immediately the dog obeyed and came to him.

Mr. Thomas looked at Deborah. "It's time for us to head back to the barn. The cows are ready for milking."

Jeremiah asked his mother. "Do you want some water brought up after we finish milking?"

"Yes, you can show Deborah the way to the river so she can get it by herself tomorrow," Mrs. Thomas said.

The young servant girl found herself heading outside to the barn. This time she wasn't alone. No more lonely days!

The dog moved beside Mr. Thomas keeping a few feet parallel to him. Jeremiah walked on the other side of his father. Her new master turned his head slightly while she kept an even pace from behind and said, "Your Uncle Nehemiah told me that he taught you to milk cows."

Deborah was pleased knowing that her Uncle Nehemiah had spoken well of her to Mr. Thomas. She answered. "Yes, sir."

Silence followed for a few seconds and then he said to her. "I also heard you can harness a horse."

Deborah remained silent remembering the massive horse in the barn. She answered him, "I need to learn; it has been a long time."

They reached the barn. Deborah noticed the horse did not look as huge as earlier that morning when she was alone. She saw beside the stall of the horse was in a pen with young lambs cuddled so close to their mother, it was difficult to see separate animals. When they saw her watching them, they leaped up, revealing more sheep and lambs than she had previously seen. Several young lambs collided against the gate separating Deborah from them. She patted their soft heads and found her hand wet from the tongues of many lovable lambs. "My, they certainly are friendly," Deborah said to herself.

She had been so excited enjoying the sheep that Mr. Thomas and his son had left her alone. "Where are they?" She wondered.

Mr. Thomas's deep voice came from the neighboring stall. "Those sheep need some water."

Up popped Jeremiah's blonde head from the same stall. He said, "Pa I can show Deborah where to get water for them."

Mr. Thomas walked out from the stall with his hand on Jeremiah's bony shoulder. "Go ahead son and show her, I can finish milking by myself."

At that point, Deborah understood Jeremiah was there to teach her about chores. Deborah followed Jeremiah; he grabbed two buckets that hung on pegs next to the door and passed one of them to her. He opened the barn door, and Shep sat eagerly outside.

"You have been a good boy, waiting for us."

Jeremiah ruffled the top of the dog's thick furry head. Shep dashed ahead of them, heading towards the woods. A squirrel scampered up the tall maple tree. Deborah said, "I think Shep must be a good hunting dog."

"He is always fast like that and we're lucky to have him," bragged Jeremiah.

Deborah thought for a moment and said with some curiosity. "My Uncle Nehemiah had a dog that looked just like Shep."

After a few minutes passed, he said, "Pa brought him home after a trip to Plymouth where he bought a few sheep. He was in the wagon curled up against the sheep sleeping. He was just a puppy."

Deborah thought for a moment and said, "My Uncle Nehemiah and his wife live in Plymouth."

Deborah's mood turned bitter as she remembered her mother and two younger siblings also live with them.

Jeremiah slapped his thigh and motioned to the dog saying, "Come, boy."

The dog moved in between the two of them as they walked on the trail side by side. Deborah noticed Jeremiah was much shorter than her. For some reason, she felt he was taller and older. He was very sure of himself. While following him on the narrowing trail, she saw he walked with a slight limp. He stopped and turned. Deborah stood, biting her lip and staring at him and though, "Cousin Ruth walked with a limp." Although Cousin Ruth never ran like Jeremiah. He had run while rescuing her from the mean chicken earlier that morning."

Jeremiah glanced back while Deborah stood still staring.

Deborah's cheeks flushed with shame realizing how long she had been staring at him.

"Are you hurt?" She asked him.

"My leg gets sore sometimes. I don't know why." He gave his shoulders a shrug.

Deborah nodded.

They continued down the trail. Deborah heard the familiar sound of rushing water. The sitting rock at the river's edge at Cousin Ruth's farm flashed across her mind. She had almost forgotten what happiness felt like until hearing the roaring water. She raised her hand to shield her eyes from the sun. A large meadow came into view.

"I hear the river," shouted Deborah.

They both raced across the meadow and ran down the embankment. Each dipped a pail into the cold water. Deborah stood on the rocky shore. Deborah's pail sloshed over the brim of her bucket with water. She looked over her shoulder, and Jeremiah had gone. He had already started up the river's embankment with his bucket filled with water. She was astonished how fast he could move despite his sore leg.

He yelled at her. "Come this way; it is not as steep."

Deborah quickly caught up to him, finding her bucket of water growing heavy.

She looked at Jeremiah struggling to carry his pale of water and said, "The Widow Thatcher had a well near her house. It was not this hard to get water."

Horrified by her comment, she swallowed hard wanting to erase her mean words.

Jeremiah did not seem to be bothered and told her. "Next time you can bring ole Sam. It will be better. Carrying these pails across the meadow can take a while without a horse. You are a stranger, and ole Sam can be mean. Once that horse gets used to seeing you, he will be as sweet as apple pie."

Deborah struck out ahead of him, mad he had not brought the horse. She fumed to herself. "I would not be afraid of an old horse."

The farmhouse rested on the top of the hill overlooking the meadow they had crossed on the way to the river. It wasn't as far as she thought. She was halfway across the field leaving Jeremiah far behind.

Jeremiah caught up to her. "I hope you are not mad. I should have brought the horse to help us."

"No," she answered, embarrassed her temper had flared.

He looked at Deborah and said, "Will you be okay getting to the house and he pointed to it up on the hill."

"Yes, I can see it."

"I better get this bucket of water to the barn; my Pa is waiting."

They both departed at the foot of the hill at the end of the trail. Jeremiah disappeared on the path to the barn. Deborah continued up the knoll to the farmhouse.

Once Deborah reached the farmhouse with the water, she was put to work helping Mrs. Thomas with cleaning and caring for the two young boys.

Deborah liked the busy Thomas household.

A 1770's homestead that could have been the Thomas's

Chapter 8: Sparks Ignite

Could it be a sin to enjoy her time spent with Richard? Deborah and Richard delivered corn to the hungry people in Boston each week, and he always escorted her back to the Thomas farm to ensure her safety. How could she take pleasure during times of suffering? Deborah decided she would look for direction in the old Bible Reverend Conant had given to her not long after she lived with Cousin Ruth. It had been eight years since Cousin Ruth had died. Deborah had learned from her that the Bible was the word of God. A memory of Cousin Ruth came to her; the image of Ruth holding up her damaged hand came alive. Ruth spoke to her. "School children have come to this house for years and I thought my life was useless after my accident. Deborah, my accident gave me the chance to teach all the children and be a mother to you!"

For a moment the memory was so vivid, it seemed Ruth was alive. She shook her head in uncertainty. "That must be it, God has sent me a revelation and is using this time I have with Richard to become his wife. It can't be a sin if

God is using our time together," Deborah reasoned with herself.

With the solution to her feelings of love, she felt convinced that someday Richard would be her husband. Deborah finished her morning chores and harnessed the horse for her weekly ride to the Leonard farm not aware that the British no longer controlled Boston. She looked in the corner of the barn where the sack of corn was usually laying against the wall. It was not there. A sudden uneasiness entered her body. Her cheeks grew warm while her keen eyes searched the barn for any movement, scanning the building for any red coated soldiers. She heard a male clear his throat from behind her, and immediately recognized it was Richard Leonard. She felt his trembling hand touch her shoulder. And Deborah turned around wondering what was wrong. Richard withdrew his hand apologizing for startling her. He told her that she no longer needed to bring food, the people of Boston were free.

Deborah kept smiling and her adoring eyes looked warmly up at Richard's face.

Uncomfortable with her overly affectionate fixation, he looked away focusing on the horse that had walked over to him. Ole Sam nuzzled his shoulder. Richard turned around and Deborah was still standing gawking at him. Richard cleared his throat and spoke. "I will miss you. And all the times we traveled back here after delivering the food. It is hard to believe we never got caught by all those redcoats scattered in the forests. I think it is about time for me to join the fight. I told my mother I have decided to enlist tomorrow. She told me I must pay a visit to the folks at the Thomas farm, but my first thought was to tell you, and my mother agreed."

Richard's news of enlisting in the Continental Army was something he had never spoke about. Her ears pounded. "Did he know how much she had grown to love him?" Somehow, she thought, he had felt affection for her too. How can our time together be lost in just one day?"

Richard broke into her thoughts. "My mother has grown fond of you. Mother would like you to do some weaving, and she will pay for your time. And I will always think of you as a loyal sister."

Deborah swallowed her romantic notions the second he called her sister. She collapsed, and he tried to catch her, but it was too late. She struck the side of her head on the stall. Immediately Richard picked her up and Deborah lay motionless in his arms. He carried her from the barn and hastened up the hill to the farmhouse.

Richard banged violently on the door. Deborah had started to wake, writhing in his arms and then turned limp.

Mrs. Thomas whisked the door open and yelled. "My Lord, poor girl!"

Deborah's limp body stiffened, and she open her eyes only to be met by Richard's frantic face and hear the fearless voice of a women telling him, "Follow me and put her on the table.

Deborah groggily gained consciousness and lifted her head, "Where am I?" She whispered.

Mrs. Thomas, perplexed, said. "Poor girl is in shock."

Richard's face turned pale. He said, "I just came to tell her that General Washington's soldiers had set the people of Boston free. I told her that I decided to join the Continental Army. She then fainted and hit her head on the horse stall."

Mrs. Thomas pursed her lips, immediately understanding Deborah's broken heart.

She hastened to the parlor table. "Lay her here."

As instructed, he put her on the large table. "What can I do?"

She promptly replied, "You may find Mr. Thomas."

Deborah moved on the table and managed to raise her head. She put her hand on the side of her head and kept it there. Red blood trickled down past her hand and onto her neck.

"What happened to me, my head hurts?"

"You fell in the barn and hit your head," said Mrs. Thomas who held the bloody cloth away and assessed her cut head.

"Oh, I remember," Deborah said while struggling to sit up.

Richard walked to the door and Deborah immediately focused on him. It flung open and Jeremiah came running past the threshold almost knocking Richard over. "Hey, slow down," Richard said grabbing him.

"Deborah needs you to be calm. She gave us a scare. Your mother is taking care of her."

Jeremiah pushed Richard back so hard he almost lost his own footing. Richard looked sadly back at him, mumbled a few words, and continued to walk out the door.

Jeremiah focused on Deborah and rushed to the parlor table where she was laying.

"Help me get her into the chair." He was told by his mother.

"What happened and why is Richard here?"

"She fell and hit her head. Right now, you be quiet and help me." She gave him a stern look.

Mrs. Thomas gently guided Deborah off the table. She put her arm around Deborah's waist and steered her into a sturdy chair that Jeremiah held firmly so it would not move. Deborah let out a sigh of relief thanking them both with a grateful glance. She held the rag to her throbbing head and remarked. "I am sorry for all the trouble."

Mrs. Thomas compassionately smiled at Deborah and placed her hand on her heart. "I thank the Lord your cut isn't deep. It is a long scrape."

Jeremiah ran to the sink and grabbed a bowl filling it with water. He gingerly walked across the room and placed the bowl on the table close to the chair where Deborah was sitting. He then ran over to the corner hutch and took out several cloths and a bottle. He returned with the items, giving them to his mother. She placed them between her and Deborah.

Jeremiah let out a cough and held his mouth. Mrs. Thomas could see he was about to be sick, "You better be quick "and she pointed toward the door.

"Mind you come back as soon as you're done," she instructed.

Deborah straightened in the chair. Mrs. Thomas tended to the abrasion on her head.

The two of them were alone. Mrs. Thomas held the side of Deborah's head and remarked to her, "By this evening you will have a sizeable lump, and I suspect your heart has been broken as well!"

Her eyes flashed wide open in horror while looking at Mrs. Thomas. Deborah gasped, "How did you know?"

"I could tell every week when you returned from delivering the food. You had a glow each time Richard escorted you back safely," she explained.

"Now I remember why I fell in the barn he told me that he had decided to enlist. And he called me a loyal sister."

"Richard carried you to the house. He told me you hit your head when you fell," said Mrs. Thomas.

"To know he thought of me as a loyal sister were feelings I was not prepared to hear. It caused me to faint and strike my head," Deborah said as her mood turned distressed.

"Were you ever misled about his intentions?" asked Mrs. Thomas.

"No mam, he never deceived me. I was shocked that he was leaving and felt nothing more than brotherly love for me. I am just a foolish girl and let my dreams about him seem genuine."

On March seventeenth, 1776, the eight-year occupation of Boston ended. General George Washington's strategy of building fortifications with cannons watching over southern Boston forced the British to flee. The ships General Howe expected to arrive with reinforcements were delayed by a ferocious storm. He felt the city would be defenseless and expose his troops to a massacre. Thousands of British soldiers and loyalists under his command would face certain death. They all set sail to Halifax Nova Scotia.

George Washington leading his men

Chapter 9: Devotion

A few days had passed since Richard Leonard's shocking departure to join General George Washington and the soldiers to fight for liberty. She felt the small lump behind her ear. She winced, the pain reminding how foolish she had been falling in love so hastily.

She lay in bed, relishing all the attention bestowed upon her after her accident. The love of the Thomas family felt wonderful. She drifted off to sleep.

Morning came. "As quick as a wink" she quietly giggled to herself.

Deborah sat upright in her bed, looked out the attic window and saw the hillside covered with a new layer of snow. Breathing in the cool air, she noticed the fogginess in front of her as she exhaled. She shuddered and wrapped her woolen shawl tightly across her shoulders. "It is too cold to remain here in the attic."

After rushing to put on another pair of woolen socks, she stood beside her bed and found her boots hurt. Plopping herself onto the bed Deborah decided the thick woolen socks caused her boots to be too tight. She began to unlace them to remove her thick socks.

The light of the early sunrise faintly filtered into the room. She noticed draped over the chest beside her bed was the shawl she had seen Mrs. Thomas crocheting. New black boots were placed near the chest.

It was Deborah's birthday. Her birthday had never been mentioned by anyone in the Thomas family. December 18th always went by like an ordinary day, but this year was different. Deborah was dumbfounded that Mrs. Thomas knew this year was special.

"I am eighteen," Deborah announced to herself and sat down on her bed. With her new boots in view, she picked them up and placed them on her lap to admire. After a few minutes, Deborah put the boots on and found they fit nicely. She stood next to her bed and discarded the old shawl she had worn for several years and placed the dark blue shawl over her shoulders. She felt warmth radiate through every part of her body. Frightened she spun around when she heard her door creak open. Mrs. Thomas stood in the doorway smiling. Deborah had never seen her look so beautiful!

A smile grew on Deborah's face, and she rushed to Mrs. Thomas. They both embraced.

Mrs. Thomas released her and spoke. "Eighteen years old," she held Deborah's chin and gazed lovingly into her grayish- blue eyes. You have become the devoted daughter I never had. And for you; today marks the end of your service to our family."

Deborah wrapped the shawl closer to her neck, grasping it for the warmth it provided and the affection she felt. "Thank you, Mrs. Thomas for everything."

Mrs. Thomas smiled and turned toward the stair landing and proceeded to descend them.

Deborah followed Mrs. Thomas down the narrow attic stairway that led to the parlor. Mrs. Thomas abruptly stopped at the entrance to the parlor and slowly spun around raising the lantern shining the light in Deborah's face. "You were just a girl the first time you climbed these steps. And now you've grown into a fine young woman."

For the first time, they entered the parlor together, Deborah felt the new bond of sharing woman hood. Deborah leaned into Mrs. Thomas and whispered, although the parlor was empty except for them. "Can we be kindred spirits just like Ruth and Naomi in the Bible?"

Mrs. Thomas face was silent. Deborah grew nervous wondering why she had dared to make such an intimate request.

"Forgive me Mrs. Thomas, I should not have asked," said Deborah.

She quickly said, "Oh no, dear it is true."

Tears glistened in Mrs. Thomas's eyes. "I never had a daughter, but you are as much like a daughter to me as Ruth was to Naomi."

"I am so thankful you are not upset that I asked this question," Deborah exhaled, and all her dread was gone after hearing the welcome response to her question.

The Revolutionary War Flag and soldier
13 stars for 13 states

Chapter 10: The Blooming Boy

Deborah was heartbroken as she watched little Sarah leave her classroom. Sarah's mother had recently died, and Sarah's aunt had brought her on the last day of summer school to say goodbye. "Good by Miss Sampson, I will miss you," Sarah said.

The little girl reminded her of her own childhood although her loss had been more complicated. Deborah's concern reflected her mood of stinging memories, deeply embedded in her mind. She had finished teaching another summer. She vowed this would be her last summer of teaching.

Deborah was fortunate to be hired at Sproat Tavern to spin cloth for new uniforms needed for the Continental soldiers. She heard so many firsthand accounts of the war at the pub while she sat spinning. The wheels constant humming put the men at ease while they spilt out their latest news of the revolutionary war. Sometimes the tavern owner Mr. Sproat, would notice

Deborah's interest in a heated conversation and clear his throat as a reminder to the patrons a female was present.

Her mindset became filled with a plan. Deborah knew that most women were already married by her age. She had no desire to marry. Her thoughts were filled with a plan to join The Continental Army. Much effort on her part alone would make her plan work to join the army to fight for the country she loved. She had no suitors interested, no attachments. She would do it but cautiously. "God help me", she prayed.

A few more days passed, and Deborah continued to spin but now instead of listening to conversations she prayed for help with her soldier's plan.

After the church service that Sunday Mr. Leonard and his wife asked Deborah if she would like to live with them. And they would provide a room for her to set up her spinning wheel to make cloth for soldier's uniforms. Deborah let out a gasp of astonishment and her gentle grey eyes sparkled with happiness and answered, "Oh yes".

The first night she arrived at the farm. They took her to their son's old bedroom. So many years had passed since Richard had broken her heart. It was difficult to lay in the same bed where he had slept many nights. She had not forgotten him.

Deborah dreamed vividly that night and woke in a sweat from a nightmare. The dream showed a trunk near her bed and Richard's mother sobbing and packing blood-stained clothes that he had worn. Deborah bolted up from her pillow and shook her head in disbelief. Darkness encompassed her as she sat in bed forgetting for a moment where she was sleeping. Lifting the quilt snug over her face, she tried to forget he was dead. The dust of daylight entered the bedroom when she lifted the covers. The trunk was located near the end of the bed as she had dreamt. At that moment, chills overtook her body. She got out of bed, dragging the quilt with her, and wrapping it around her body. Curiosity conquered her fear, and she edged toward the end of the bed. She saw the trunk.

Deborah struggled to open it and almost gave up. She screamed to herself, "it is locked! Why, why, I am so close."

A small thud hit the wall behind her. Deborah rushed to the window. She peeked through the curtains, and down below in the snow was the tiny lifeless body of a bird. Then, while turning her head, she saw a key dangling from a nail on the window frame.

"The key must open it."

Anticipation filled her with excitement. Deborah grabbed the key and was ready to open the locked trunk. She struggled to open the old finicky lock. Slowly she maneuvered the key. Click, click, and the lid began to rise. She almost stopped herself from inspecting his clothes. Hesitating, feeling like an intruder, she stood motionless. Then, for a few seconds of mulling over her plan of being a soldier, clarity returned. Her stomach grew queasy as she lifted his old uniform shirts. Some pants were underneath them. His clothes were perfect patterns to make herself soldier's clothes. Tears uncontrollably filled her eyes. She drew Richard's shirt to her face and dapped her tear-filled eyes. She gently shut the lid of the trunk, leaving most of his things undisturbed. Deborah went to the window and put the key back on the nail. Deborah closed her eyes and thanked God for the help. She looked down to see that the little bird was gone.

The days were becoming longer, which gave Deborah ample time each evening to finish sewing clothes for Robert Shurtleffe. The name she had chosen to use to enroll in the Continental Army.

She enlisted in the Spring and was nicknamed that blooming boy since shaving was not needed.

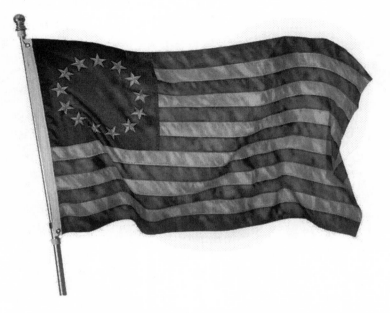

What Deborah Sampson chose to fight for, our
American Revolutionary War

From The Desk of The Author

I came upon the story of Deborah Sampson as I researched my Longfellow family roots. After finishing my family history, Deborah's story remained on my mind.

Very little has been written about females and their contributions to early American history. I decided to write this book to show children what a poor farm girl did to help create freedom. Deborah sought education and persevered through many setbacks.

Photography Notes

The photographs in this book were taken by the author or sampled from the internet. They have all have been enhanced and put through a grey tone filter.

About The Author

Pam Archambault has written several devotionals, stories, published poetry and Christmas Church play. Formerly a dental assistant, and prayer ministry leader. She played the violin and alto sax. Pam spent her childhood summers in Maine. Her grandparents generously hosted her family at their cottage in Gardiner. She is a cancer survivor.

Pam was born in Menominee, Michigan. She and her husband, Patrick, have one grown daughter Amy. Connecticut is their home.

Made in the USA
Middletown, DE
27 September 2023